CAN DO

Familiar Things

Books in the series:

 Familiar Things
by Sally Thomas

 Eco–Ventures
by Hannah Sugar, Kids' Clubs Network

 Serious Fun: Games for 4–9s
by Phill Burton, Dynamix

 Whatever the Weather
by Jane Gallagher

 Cool Creations
by Mary Allanson, Kids' Clubs Network

 Serious Fun: Games for 10–14s
by Phill Burton, Dynamix

 Sticks and Stones
by Sharon Crockett

Series Foreword

Children and young people of all ages should be able to initiate and develop their own play. Adult involvement should be based on careful observation, appropriate consultation and response to what the children need in terms of their development at this time and in this place.

Play is freely chosen personally directed behaviour motivated from within. Adults can create the best possible conditions for play: the time, space, materials, safety and support for children to develop the skills and understanding they need to extend the possibilities of their play. The degree to which the children and young people are able to make any activity their own will determine its success as a play opportunity rather than simply 'entertainment', a means of 'keeping them busy' or producing 'something to take home to parents'.

Many of the ideas in these books are not new. Indeed play games and creative activities are passed on across many generations and between different cultures across the world, constantly being adapted and changed to suit a new time, a new group of children, a new environment.

We have acknowledged sources and sought permission wherever it has been possible to do so. We hope, and indeed anticipate, that the ideas in these books will be adapted and developed further by those that use them and would be very interested to hear your comments, thoughts, ideas and suggestions.
www.thomsonlearning.co.uk/childcare

Annie Davy

CAN DO
Familiar Things

By **Sally Thomas**
Series Editor: **Annie Davy**

THOMSON

Australia • Canada • Mexi... ...ited Kingdom • United States

THOMSON

Familiar Things

Copyright © Sally Thomas 2002

The Thomson logo is a registered trademark used herein under licence.

For more information, contact Thomson, High Holborn House, 50–51 Bedford Row, London, WC1R 4LR or visit us on the World Wide Web at: http://www.thomsonlearning.co.uk

British Library Cataloguing–in–Publication Data
A catalogue record for this book is available from the British Library

ISBN 1-86152-837-X

First edition 2002

Typeset by Bottle & Co., Banbury, UK

Printed in Croatia by Zrinski

Text design by Bottle & Co.

Contents

Getting to know familiar things

What does it do?

'Me and my world'

Just a cardboard box

Just Pretending

Just for a laugh

Series Introduction

The CAN DO series is an intensely practical resource for children who attend childcare settings, drop in centres or playsettings out of school, and for those of you who work with them in these settings. Anyone working with children, whether as a trainee, an experienced manager or as a volunteer will sometimes get tired, feel jaded or simply seek new inspiration. Whether you are a childminder, a playworker, a family centre worker or a day nursery assistant or manager, you will find a rich source of ideas for children of all ages in the CAN DO series. In these books you will find practical answers to the difficult 'CAN DO' questions which are often asked of adults working with children:

- Child coming in from school, 'What can I do today?'
- Parent visiting a childminder: 'What exactly can the children do here?'
- Playworker or Childcare worker at a team meeting: 'What can we do to extend the range of play provision here?'

The series is structured towards 3 different age ranges— 0–3, 4–9 and 10–14, but many of the books will be used successfully by or with older or younger children. The books are written by authors with a wide range of experience in working with children and young people, and who have a thorough understanding of the value of play and the possibilities and constraints of work in childcare and play settings.

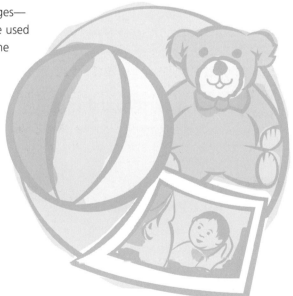

Each activity is introduced with a 'why we like it' section, which explains why children and adults who work with children have found this to be something that they enjoyed, or that has enhanced their play provision. Many of the activities also have 'Snapshots' and 'Spotlight' boxes which expand on the possibilities as developed by children, or an approach you can take in working with children. These sections are intended to help you reflect on your work and the quality of what is provided.

The ideas in this series are intended to be playful, inclusive and affordable. They are not based on any prescribed curriculum, but they could be used to enrich and develop almost any setting in which children play and learn. They do not rely on expensive toys and equipment; they are environmentally friendly and are peppered with practical tips and health and safety checkpoints.

Language used in the book

SETTING: We have used the term 'setting' rather than drop in centre, nursery, creche, etc. as the generic term to describe the range of contexts for childcare and work with young children and parents, including childminders' homes. 'Snapshots' draw on a range of different settings to illustrate the development of some of the activities in practice.

CARER: This is the term used predominantly in the 0–3s series as this is the most familiar generic term which covers adults working with children in this age range

Familiar Things

Introduction

The title of this book in the Can Do series is not just an important clue to its contents, but is a reminder of the very crucial need for babies and very young children to be cared for by loving and familiar adults in a nurturing and familiar environment.

Effective teachers in schools know that their pupils of all ages fare best when meeting a new challenge if it can be related to the skills and knowledge which the children and young people already have.

Travel agents report that their most popular hotels in exotic and unfamiliar locations are those where the owners speak some English. Most of us feel easiest embarking on a new course if we already know some of the participants, or we sign up for a beginners French class, after several years of learning it at school, because we feel more confident that we shall manage it.

If this need for a helping of the 'known' with the 'unknown' is important for adults, it is even more so for babies and very young children. In fact the size of the 'familiar' helping needs to be considerably bigger than the 'unfamiliar' portion. Playing with and watching babies we see that they often settle for about 80% familiar to 20% new for confident and sustained play.

When they have a meaningful grasp of language the proportion gradually changes to about 70% familiar to 30% new, and it stays there until the children are seven or eight years old and doesn't change much even after that.

Adults who have newly arrived in a child's environment will greatly help the child, and themselves, if they regard themselves as that 20–30% new and become familiar by staying warmly alongside known carers and activities whilst being gradually absorbed into the child's world.

Awareness of this aspect of caring for a child from birth to four years not only sustains that child's emotional well being but will set up a lifelong positive attitude towards people and settings beyond the immediate family, as well as towards new experiences and discoveries.

You will find that the activities in this book start with what is already known and familiar and add new ideas or materials to encourage children and their carers to enjoy developing their play.

Acknowledgements for *Familiar Things*

The author would like to thank the following people:

The wealth of authors who continue to inspire me, perhaps especially Sara Meadows. Kenneth Kaye and Urie Bronfenbrenner

Elinor Goldshmeid and Sonia Jackson for introducing the treasure baskets into day–care in their book *People under Three*

The students I taught on the Diploma in Nursery Nursing course at Oxford College of Further Education between 1990 and 1998 for their commitment and enthusiasm in providing rewarding play opportunities for 0–3s both then, and now as practitioners

The children and staff of OCFE Day Nursery on the Blackbird Leys site, and those of OXFAM Workplace Day Nursery, for providing some of the photographs for this book

Vicky Hamlet for her willingness and word-processing skills

Annie Davy for her invaluable help and advice

To my grown up children and their children for all they have taught and are still teaching me

You and Me, and Maybe One or Two Others

Faces, hands and heartbeats: the first treasure collection (birth onwards)

Why we like it

Babies are born with a ready-made treasure collection in the shape of their mum. At birth they are already familiar with her voice and heartbeat and they spend the following weeks watching her face, feeling her skin and her hands, accompanied by that reassuring voice and heartbeat which are never far away.

Watching her face

Feeling her skin

What you might need

Just you.

How you can do it

This treasure collection doesn't need to be wound up to work—in fact it works best if it isn't! It moves and smiles, nuzzles, talks and sings little tunes of its own accord, comes close, then moves further away. It is familiar yet subtly different every time. The baby absorbs all of it. It is the most stimulating and encouraging plaything of all, and it can set up warm feelings towards new experiences from now on.

Other people in daily caring contact with a baby—dads, other family members, nannies, childminders or day nursery staff—need to pick up on some of these familiar anchors to establish their own close relationships and provide babies with *their* treasure collections.

Here are a few pointers that may help.

A baby in the first few weeks focusses best on a face that is quite near (about 22 cm away), so cradling in your arms to comfort or to bottle feed gives the baby a chance to watch you closely and get to know you.

As the field of vision extends the baby will be able to see you clearly from further away, and dressing and changing times are valuable for making loving relationships when your talking, smiling, stroking and singing let the baby know that this is a good place to be.

In the first few weeks a baby will focus best on a face that is quite close

Singing is really important. Rhythms that mimic our heartbeats are there in our Nursery rhymes, baby songs and lullabies, and singing while gently patting can hold interest and soothe a baby at the same time. It doesn't matter if you can't hold a tune—the baby loves a sing-song voice. Those traditional baby songs sung by everyone caring for a baby soon becomes a familiar thing that binds all the carers together and provides comfort and security.

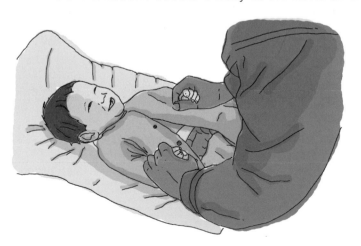

Changing times are valuable for making loving relationships

Singing is really important, and it binds carers together

What next?

Soon the baby will be able to use you as a support cushion, resting back against you feeling the warmth of your body and hearing your voice while clutching your fingers.

Now interest will begin to focus on other nearby things, your watch perhaps, or another child coming close, a toy held by you or a mobile moving in the breeze.

From this point it is a very small step to introducing a treasure basket of everyday objects that the baby can explore with you.

Soon the baby will be able to clutch your fingers, while using you as a cushion

What's This?

Exploring familiar things (2$^{1}/_{2}$–6 months)

Why we like it

Elinor Goldschmied and Sonia Jackson in their wonderful book *People Under Three* introduce treasure basket play for babies in day care who can sit steadily but are not yet on the move, and who need absorbing exploratory activities that are supported by 'attentive but non-intrusive adults'.

I find that those treasure basket ideas can be adapted to engage even younger babies, who naturally need much more adult support.

This activity begins from the time a baby can comfortably 'prop' against you on the floor with your legs forming a 'v' shaped pillow for all round support.

Snapshot

Foster Mum, with Tessie (just 3 months), is holding a neck scarf she had just taken off:

'Oh, do you like that then? Is that just what you've always wanted?'

She brings it closer to the baby's face:

'I can see you—yes I can!

Look it's waving, waving to Tessie!

Do you want to hold it Tessie?

There you are, cuddle, cuddle your scarf'.

She comments to her friend: 'It probably smells of me—I took it off because I was hot!'

But of course Tessie will like it all the better if it does.

What you might need

Soft floor covering (such as sheepskin perhaps)

Something comfortable for you to lean against such as the front of a sofa or some floor cushions against the wall. (An uncomfortable adult won't be able to stay the course or be happily involved with the baby.)

A low soft basket (I use those French cotton breadbaskets that tie together in all four corners)

A choke tester from an Early Learning Centre just to make sure

Contents for the basket (these are just suggestions):

Two or three things that are already familiar (the crinkley ball or rag doll that goes everywhere, or perhaps the soft rubbery spoon that normally goes with apple sauce)

A soft adult glove with 2 or 3 round sleigh bells dropped inside, and then machine stitched across

A wooden pastry brush with a small rounded handle and soft bristles, or a soft baby's hair brush

A square of crinkley paper (from inside a box of chocolates)

A well made key ring with 2 or 3 keys and a soft fob (for example, a leather flower).

A small chiffon scarf or familiar lengths of Sari material

Baby slippers

A round un-breakable camping mirror

A laminated photo of mum or dad

A small plastic jar with something that rattles (for example, a necklace, or bangles, or buttons, or a few coloured pasta shells) The jar should have a screw-on lid either glued on or re-inforced with stretch Elastoplast from a reel, wound round the join

Nothing is excluded, but think about safety. Even though you are going to be there all the time, you don't want to have to be suddenly negative. Leave out brightly coloured plastic or garish items as these can be very tiring to look at for long.

The baby's attention will let you know if the object is liked

How you can do it

For the youngest babies it will be your hands that pick up the objects whilst they wave their hands in the vicinity and 'swipe' at the object. This means that you will be choosing what to pick, but don't let this reduce the baby's choice. The baby's attention, eyes and body movements will let you know whether or not the object is liked, so pay close attention to the signals sent out.

With very young babies don't be afraid to `chat along` interpreting the baby's interest.

What next?

This is a positive experience for babies before they can sit unaided as it helps them to associate being on the floor with being happy and engaged. They also see that the adults enjoy being down there too—which is important if a little later on we are going to expect them to spend some time on the floor without adult support.

The activity, of course, leads on to the better known treasure basket play which is described in detail by Goldschmied and Jackson and which occupies babies so successfully between 5, or 6, and 9 months.

The better known treasure basket

Where's It Gone?

Making and playing with posting boxes (9 months–2 years)

Why we like it

This activity grows with babies and toddlers from the time they can pull themselves up to stand until they are about two years old. You can gradually adapt and add to the basic box to encourage new skills and understanding, by adding new objects, or using a different approach with the familiar ones, as you go along.

What you might need

A strong bottomless cardboard box about 45 cm high and roughly 30 x 30 cm in other directions

A Stanley knife

Parcel or electrician's tape

A torch or bike light

A basket or low container of everyday objects such as key rings with old keys, little tins or boxes, a pastry brush, spoons or postcards.

Spotlight

At 9 months babies will use the posting box to practise what they understand about object permanence (that is realising that mum or teddy is still somewhere even when they can't be seen). This is why games of 'Boo' are very popular at this age, and the game 'Where's it gone?' of hiding and finding things in a posting box is enjoyed for the same reason. This activity also helps 9 month olds to practise letting go of what they are holding. The instinct to hold on tight is very strong and at this age the babies will often put something in your hand and take it back again without ever uncurling their fingers! So you may find the spoon is posted through the hole and then brought out again by the same route. Some babies may bang the object to release their grip on it, in which case it may end up on top of the box!

How you can do it

1. Cut 1 or 2 holes in each side of the box. Don't worry about the shape, but make sure most of them are big enough to take most objects.

2. Stick parcel tape around the holes if the cardboard is at all rough.

3. Make additional peepholes on top to shine the torch through.

Snapshot

The carer in a day nursery is kneeling and looking through a hole of the posting box:

'There's Rabbit! Look Daisy, I can see your rabbit.' Daisy (10 months) crawls over and tries to pull off the carer's glasses. Carer laughs 'Not my glasses Daisy—look! in here'. She turns on a bike light on top of the box and light shining through the hole catches Daisy's attention. She moves off the carer's knee and grasps the hole to look inside.

The carer spends 10 minutes helping Daisy to post Rabbit and retrieve it by tipping up the box.

(Interestingly Daisy lets go of Rabbit each time the carer says 'Bang!')

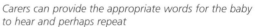

Carers can provide the appropriate words for the baby to hear and perhaps repeat

What next?

The posting box gives lots of opportunities for close interaction between babies and carers. Look for the baby demonstrating understanding by use (that is, picking up the mug and pretending to drink, or the brush to brush hair or teeth, or the floor). Carers can provide the appropriate words for the baby to hear and perhaps repeat, as well as surprised looks and smiling enthusiasm for the game.

As the babies toddle more steadily they enjoy games that give them good reasons for purposeful toddling. Filling a shopping trolley or baby cart with their choice of things and then transporting them across the room to post involves several skills, which can be repeating all over again if you move the box to another part of the room.

Another One!

Searching and matching games for toddlers (14 months–4 years)

Why we like it

Recognising that 2 objects are identical comes early, usually around the same time as babies are able to toddle a short way on their own. It was probably an essential skill for survival in times when the search was for edible things, and you needed to make sure you had got the same as everyone else. That close interest in what the other child has is still very evident in most under threes, who only relax when they see that they have one too!

These searching and matching activities will need to be led by you at first. Later you can support the same skills by adapting the posting box in various ways. The final tray version is enjoyed by children from around three onwards.

What you might need

For all these activities you will need collections of several of each object (identical objects for under threes, and very similar ones for threes to fours)

You could use teaspoons, sample computer discs, lolly sticks, pencils, stock cube boxes or similar, combs, mittens, socks, patterned paper napkins, fir-cones, shuttlecocks, model animals from a farm or wildlife set, small wooden blocks of one colour, dolly pegs, plastic eggs, etc.

Add more items as indicated for each 'stage' of the activity.

How you can do it

1. You will need a tabard or overall for you to wear with a big pocket. Hide, in a fairly obvious way, all of the objects except one of each. Put those in your overall pocket and let the child choose one. Set off to search together for the things that match it.

2. Use the posting box and a skewer to make 2 pinholes next to each posting hole.

Thread a length of round elastic through the pinholes and tie a loop. Try fastening an object in the elastic loop by a posting hole. As matching objects are found they can be posted, and the number of them exclaimed over at the end. 2 or 3 toddlers may enjoy playing this game at the same time.

3. Later, with the posting box, use:

Postcard size squares of clear plastic fastened as 'windows' next to each posting hole, using 2 cm tape on three sides.

Photographs of everyday objects from your setting

or

Drawings of everyday objects

or

Small colour cards

Slot in, for instance, a photo of the horse from the catalogue advertising your farm set, and encourage the children to find the model horses to post in that hole. To make a colour recognition game, slot a square of the chosen colour in the 'window' and encourage the children to find something (anything) that matches it. Remember that most threes can only identify one feature at a time and so they would find a request for something for instance 'round and blue', frustrating.

The tray game

Use a tea tray or similar and 2–3 small punnets—the sort that normally hold soft fruit or small new potatoes.

Select 2 groups of items (for example, cotton reels and teaspoons) and muddle them up on a tray. Encourage the child to sort the 2 groups into the 2 punnets. You can increase the groups of objects and number of punnets as the child becomes more skilled, or suggests this. This game is very calming and satisfying for a child that has been frightened or upset, as it is reassuringly repetitive and achievable.

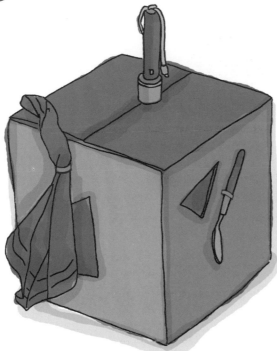

FASTEN OBJECTS TO THE POSTING
BOX, USING THE ELASTIC LOOPS
NEAR THE POSTING HOLES

Spotlight

If you are working with a mixed age range of children, these activities are ones which older children often enjoy organising for younger ones. They can be played indoors or out.

Lots of matching and sorting activities happened routinely in the days of larger families and a less hectic lifestyle. It is worth remembering that sorting the washing, the cutlery drawer, the contents of the button box, shoes and socks into pairs, apples into boxes, onions into sets, and oddments of wool into balls were really useful activities that earned real praise for children. Including these in place of play versions whenever possible will, as almost all responsibilities do, help the child's feelings of self-worth to grow.

Where Does This Go?

Making choices and grouping things together (2–4 years)

Why we like it

This type of activity has all the ingredients for involving children and letting them develop the play in their own way.

It is based on familiar things, provides lots of choice and encourages very young children to talk to you as they explore. It gives you a chance to relax and enjoy their ideas.

What you might need

Collections of objects that can be sorted in different ways, for example:

Things found in the bathroom

All red or blue or green objects

All wood or metal or paper items

Things from the seaside

Items associated with a celebration (perhaps Chinese New Year, a wedding, christmas or a Birthday)

Somewhere comfortable to explore and return to the collection (a rug or cushions).

Things from the seaside

Something for children to put their favourites in (small bags, baskets or sand buckets)

Relevant photographs of any occasions enjoyed by the children that are included in the collections, or perhaps posters of views to help them to remember what they saw or did on a particular outing.

How you can do it

You might want to set out a collection of wood items before going to watch a carpenter at work or to visit some woodland, or lay out the range of different fruits after going to the market and before making a fruit salad. A mixture of materials for children to stroke, squeeze and compare will help them to enjoy a variety of textures.

Vary the ways you introduce these opportunities to explore and let the children take the initiative at times. Sometimes they will enjoy repeating their treasure basket experiences by finding something that appeals to them, and carers can learn a lot from the associations made by very young children.

Snapshot

Mai (3 years old) chose a gymnastics baton with streamers and danced her way round the room dipping and weaving while holding it on her head. 'Oh Mai' said her keyworker entranced 'Are you being the New Year Dragon?'

'No' said Mai 'a dusty bluebell.'

Spotlight

If you have the space for a tall chest of drawers, a collection of items organised into likely categories means that you can lay hands on objects for a particular child or interest very quickly, or raid something from every drawer for a mixed collection, or produce a whole drawer of hats at the drop of one! Of course the objects don't fit just one category—a piece of driftwood might be in 'seaside' or 'wood' or 'old' or 'smooth', but it makes a useful starting point.

Try to get everyone involved in adding to your collections—grandparents, students and siblings are great sources of ideas and materials.

What next?

If the objects are left out, the children will go back and play with them again in different ways. For instance, the shell explored in the morning might be taken to be a boat on the water later on, and then as a bowl for the doll's cornflakes. Having this opportunity to play with ideas is more important than having stacks of expensive equipment, and realising that things can be grouped in different ways is a valuable piece of learning.

Shake, Rattle and Roll

Sound and movement for crawling babies (5–12 months)

Why we like it

Babies who are on the move, or nearly on the move, need the floor to be as interesting a place as possible. Of course the most interesting plaything to have down there with them is *you*, and seeing you sitting on the floor while they pad about encourages the idea that the floor is a great place to be. But when their carers need to be doing things at a higher level then babies need playthings are full of interest.

These shake, rattle and rollers are cheap, quick to make and to change, and engage babies with a variety of sound, sight and movement.

What you might need

The smallest size of plastic water bottles (round or straight sided)

A reel of stretch elastoplast

Oddments of brightly coloured paper (for example, gift paper, sweet wrappers, offcuts of holographic paper) Christmas glitter, sequins, bright buttons, bits of ribbon, and beads

A jelly cube or two

Dried peas, beans, butter beans, lentils, macaroni, etc.

How you can do it

The clear plastic bottles work best, but some small ones that are tinted blue or green can be very successful if the contents are bright enough.

1. Fill some of the bottles $^1/_4$–$^1/_3$ with water and leave others dry.

2. Put a small handful of different items in each bottle.

3. Mix up a cube of jelly so that it will only just set, and pour it into one of the bottles before it does. (Some contents, such as jelly, will go off after a time, so those bottles will need rinsing and replacing regularly.)

4. Screw the caps on tightly and bind elastoplast firmly round the join. You could also put PVA glue round the inside of the cap before screwing it on, but in my experience tightly bound stretch elastoplast defeats the most determined under one year old.

The smallest size water bottle is still quite heavy for a six month old baby to pick up, but they roll along in a very satisfactory way when batted with a hand. Older babies enjoy shaking them to music.

Snapshot

At one day nursery all of the baby room staff take responsibility for making or renewing a bottle shaker on a regular basis. They have enough to provide a 'heap' of choice for all the carers and babies to use to accompany 'Peter plays with one hammer', etc. Because the bottles are bottom heavy they also make very satisfying contents for a toddle truck for a baby who is just walking as they knock together and rattle without falling over as they are pushed along.

Peter plays with 2 hammers

Size Matters!

Hats and shoes for everyone (2–4 years)

Why we like it

These activities provide plenty of opportunities to explore and discuss bigness and smallness in a relaxed way. As with most play situations for this age group, the adult playing sympathetically alongside as an ideal playmate is enormously valuable. If he or she can enhance the play without taking it over the child will see ways of developing games, both when playing alone and with peers.

What you might need

For a shoe shop

A selection of shoes, boots, flip-flops, slippers etc., some of which are too big for some of the adults who play and a number of which are too small for the youngest children taking part

A length of wall or something to arrange them along

A couple of chairs or stools

Coins and a cash register if you like, although many 2 year olds prefer just to tap hands to give or receive money, and find the props a distraction

A foot measure laid out sideways as illustrated over page. Start with the outline of a newborn's foot if possible and continue up to a fisherman's wader size.

How you can do it

Follow the child's lead about who is the shopkeeper and who is the customer, but the child will almost certainly want to be an adult in either role.

Adult tries on a pair of baby's shoes ('But I really want to wear these... Are you sure they are too small?'). Respectful discussions with madam or sir as you work through the shoes to find a pair that fits will be equally enjoyed.

A hat shop can follow the same lines as above but is more likely to include conversations about wanting to be a postman or driver from the hat chosen.

Spotlight

One of the frustrations of being 2 or 3 years old is that you are often confronted with being big or small, and that the adults never seem to say the same things twice. Some things, like feeding yourself, are expected because you are so big and others, like holding hands on busy pavements, because you are small. It's enough to cause an outburst, and probably does!

The problem arises for young children because our descriptions of age and size are all comparative and are the result of widening experiences over many years. Remember when somebody of twenty was really old? We know what we mean by 'a huge spider,' until we go to South America that is, and that isn't the same 'huge' as for a dinosaur! Children need lots of hands-on experience and understanding conversations with their carers to begin to sort it all out.

One For You and One For You

Having fun with one-to-one correspondence–(2$\frac{1}{2}$–4 years)

Why we like it

This game puts the child firmly in power as the 'parent' ensuring equal amounts for all, whilst practising one-to-one correspondence.

What you might need

Up to 4 or 5 teddies, dolls or toy animals sitting in a circle on the floor

A shelf or box which the child can use with an assortment of paper or plastic cups, plates, picnic cutlery, straws, napkins, etc.—at least 4 or 5 of each

Enough items of plastic or real food in a bowl for one each. (Plastic items could be a hardboiled egg, tomato, pear, and real food could include grapes, carrot sticks, apple quarters, mini rice cakes, etc.)

A small teapot or jug of water.

Snapshot

Dealing things out fairly is a useful social skill as well as an important part of understanding mathematics. Watch adults agonising over a box of chocolates to see both skills in action. 'There's only one hazelnut whirl.... Does anyone mind if I take that? There'll be another one on the lower layer, but that's not fair when there are enough to go around on this top one...' 5 year olds sharing out Malteesers will give the remaining ones to mum rather than have extra ones for just some of the children.

How you can do it

Suggest a picnic or party for 'Elmer' or 'Pooh' and his friends, then stand back! Stay in the vicinity to suggest a cloth if water gets spilt, and to praise the child for giving something to everyone.

If the child is very keen for you to join the party it's fine to accept the invitation, but perhaps not such a good idea to suggest that you do. This age group enjoy being 'in charge,' and having a grown up the circle can sometimes discourage them from taking that role themselves—so if you are involved follow the child's lead and stay subordinate yourself.

This is a game that children often enjoy repeating for several days.

Dealing out helps a child understand the concept of taking turns

Spotlight

Dealing out also helps this age group to understand taking turns and they need plenty of opportunities to practise this in their play. Lining up the cars to go down the ramp, putting each horse in its own stable, and finding a cushion for storytime all help. It will probably take another 2 or 3 years before they can share out un-equal possessions or tasks using sophisticated skills of negotiation. Their first efforts may be less than tactful, ('My dad will hit your dad if you don't...', 'I won't let you come to my party' etc.) before they refine the skill ('You went first last time so...', 'I chose the video so you can choose the TV programme'). By this time they may suggest subdividing or fractions and 'owing you one', and are probably ready for those mathematical processes too!

Photographs for Choosing, Storytelling and Snap!

(Birth–3 years)

Why we like it

There is no doubt that photographs have totally changed the way we can recall events in our lives and help children to remember and enjoy all their special times, and much later on to share those with their own families. Living history is alive and well—it's just a pity that, in the rush, the camera or film often gets forgotten!

Photographs are one of the ways that parents, and other adults who care for their children, can make close links, share experiences and value the time that children spend with others.

What you might need

Photos
A camera to take lots more
Card
Access to a laminator
A hole punch.

Useful Tips

It is probably well worth investing in a digital camera and scanner if you can afford one.

Getting photos developed is not cheap. However costs can be reduced. Post-away photo services are invariably cheaper than high street prices, especially if you get two or more prints at the time of ordering, and get enlarged prints.

Most parents would love to buy a print or the negative and you can cover your costs this way.

How you can do it

Ideas for children under 1 year old

Mount some photos of familiar faces on thick card and punch 2 holes near the top. Push the base of the card between the mattress and the side of a small baby's crib and tie the top firmly around the bars.

As the baby gets bigger you could hang the photos on the wall, or fasten them back-to-back and make a mobile for the baby to wake up to.

Once the baby is crawling you could screw a length of plastic covered curtain wire along the top of the skirting board and slot the mounted photos behind. Babies will enjoy tugging them out and examining them, and the pictures make the room at floor level a much more interesting place!

Familiar faces

Ideas for children ages 1–4

Do all you can to get the use of a laminator. A local school or business might be persuaded to let you use theirs at cost, or a parent may have access to one. Laminated photographs make great place mats, and toddlers love finding themselves at mealtimes. 2 or 3 photos laminated in an A4 size mat provides plenty of interest whilst their lunch is being served.

Try taking photos of any sequence of events, for example: looking out of the window on a wet day, pulling on boots, zipping anorak, putting up an umbrella; splashing in the puddles. Once laminated, these can be arranged and re-arranged, and used to encourage the children's conversation.

Where's bubble gone

Snapshot

Zoe (2 years, 7 months) looks at a sequence of bubble-blowing photographs, 'That's me and my boots and mummy's going 'Whooo'.
'There, she's done it, and I'm dancing, dancing'
'Where's the bubble gone?'
'My turn now!'

If you laminate 2 prints of each picture the children will be able to play Pairs or Snap, or you could hide one of each in the garden and help the children to hunt for the matching ones.

What next?

Toddlers and very young children also enjoy decorating the walls with their favourite photographs. Unroll a length of 'Gripping Stuff' (sold in DIY stores for displaying Christmas cards) at the children's height along the wall. Pictures stay put just by being pressed against it, and the Gripping Stuff leaves no trace when it is peeled off.

Using Photos to Make Books for Babies

(4 months–3 years)

Why we like it

Photos like mirrors, fascinate babies:

'That's me ... Isn't it?'

'There's Mum... But she's here too.'

'There's my bottle, bear, buggy, brother.'

Looking at the very same face or toy or view that the baby already knows and loves calls for much staring and patting and smiling, and a huge desire to open a book and study the contents has begun. If that makes encouraging a love of books sound pretty easy, it is because it is. When a baby's first books are filled with pictures of everything that is personal and important to the baby, those books will become important and loved possessions to share as well as to explore alone.

What you might need

Photos

Sharp knife

Scissors

Small scrap book

PVA glue

Ribbon.

Snapshot

When I played this with several 18–21 month olds, one page had a photo of five buggies in a row but each toddler found their own!

How you can do it

Don't be too ambitious when planning a book. Several simple books made quickly will give enormous pleasure, and they can be added to easily. Making a special book about a particular holiday or occasion is dealt with in the next chapter, but here are some ideas for more everyday ones.

A good one to start with for a baby is 'who is in here?'. Glue photos of favourite people doing usual things (like making a bottle, saying hello, eating supper, looking up from playing) in the middle of every other page of a small scrapbook. Don't forget to include some of the baby.

Cut a door or window or a gate shape on the page before each photo. Make the opening slightly smaller than that photograph. PVA glue the surrounding paper on to the photo page, leaving just the window or door to open and close.

Write a very simple text that gets repeated on each page, for example:

'Knock, Knock! Who's there? It's Jamal. Hallo Jamal.'

An older child could add a letterbox, house number, curtains etc. with felt pens or scraps, and the opening parts could be strengthened with Sellotape if you like.

Ideas for extending use of baby books

Cut around a whole body picture of each baby or toddler to attach with ribbon to the spine of the book.

Strengthen the cut- outs with Sellotape. Fill an album with photos of familiar things and show the child how to use their personal cut-out to:

Play in the garden

Sit in the buggy

Lie in the cot

Look in the fridge

Climb in the highchair

Swing on the swing

Go down the slide etc.

If you look after several toddlers, keep their photos on ribbons in a wallet at the back of the book and tie on the relevant one.

A simple text is easily repeated

For two and three year olds, try using those cheap ring bound photo albums where you peel and replace a plastic sheet over the pictures. They make great storybooks if you add some speech bubbles. This isn't to teach the baby to read but so that the same familiar phrases can be used by all the adults who explore the book with the child.

Draw a page of different sized speech bubbles pointing in different directions, and photocopy it several times so that you've always got spares. Use them to make a story with any sequence of pictures.

Paul, Anouskha and every child in that sequence of events will enjoy hearing their story over and over again.

Snapshot

Zoe (4 years) looks at the picture of herself when 2 years swinging on her mum's lap: 'Was Sophie a little baby then?'

'No Sophie was still growing in mummy's tummy and you were mummy and daddy's only little girl.'

'I'm swinging a *little* bit high aren't I? I'm saying 'Come on mum—swing high like Kathryn' but Sophie is saying, 'No, no I'm too small to swing. Because I was getting *big* then... to do *big* things, but Sophie couldn't do any of them, because she couldn't see what to do, and she was getting ready to be a tiny baby.'

What next?

As the children get older they will add more details to the story and use a wider vocabulary.

Do You Remember? and That's Me!

Storybooks (2–4 years)

Why we like it

There is a lot of benefit in using our awareness of what may become memorable for the child from 'here and now' happenings, and of recording these in a book for the child to look through in years to come, with that smiling pleasure we still get when we come across a particular photograph from the past. The very fact that it was recorded acknowledges the warmth and joy of that time and supports the child's own self esteem.

A 'That's Me' book that celebrates all the positive things about being 2 or 3 years old is sometimes very helpful for a child coping with a new baby at home.

A holiday book can also serve this purpose of a positive self–image, and is perhaps especially valuable if the child is visiting far away relatives but is too young to have more than a hazy memory of the time spent with them.

What you might need

A peel back photo album or a scrapbook

A page of speech bubbles

Ephemera from the special occasion for example, tickets, the programme, a lolly stick, publicity leaflet, feather, piece of seaweed, etc.)

Photographs

A drawing or 'treasure' chosen by the child.

How you can do it

These books come alive if you stick in, not just photographs, but the leaf you found, the drawing, the bus ticket, the sweet wrapper, etc. The items can be stuck in the book beside a relevant photograph. Write a speech bubble recording what the child or carer said.

Small items that cannot be stuck in the book could be put in a purse and tied with ribbon to the binding of the album.

Ephemera from special occasions can make these books come alive

Snapshot

A special book could be made by a childminder for a child's final term in her full-time care.

- Nina and Angela went to the station and saw the express train going to Devon. 'I'll remember this,' said Nina.
- We went to watch the big children in their school concert. 'We'll remember this,' said Angela and Nina.
- Nina drew a wonderful picture for Angela 'I'll remember this' said Angela.

Snapshot

Family centre workers might make a book for a family moving away from the area, that also demonstrates the approach and value they have for all family members using their setting. With the family's permission an additional copy could be kept in the centre. Maybe something along the lines of:

When the Clark family move to their new house we shall say:

If only ____ was here to build a town with the bricks

If only ____ was here to make us all a cup of tea

If only ____ was here to sing 'Humpty Dumpty' three times with all the actions

If only ____ was here to think of some new menus

If only ____ was here to climb on the logs until his dad says 'Watch out!'

'Goodbye and Good Luck' to all the Clarks from everyone at Park End's Open Door.

Spotlight

Adults who care for babies and very young children are very aware of significant happenings for them. It is an important part of the job and we often plan to take them somewhere or introduce them to something because we see that it is 'about the right time'. We also know when one phase is coming to an end and another is about to begin—'soon you'll be a big sister' or 'after Christmas you'll be a nursery school boy'. Sometimes perhaps we anticipate too much. Preparations for going to school for instance can mean that the weeks before aren't relished and valued as much as they could be, and a child can end up being always 'pre' the next phase, for example, sleeping through, being mobile, becoming dry, etc. Even though we need to keep one eye on the future, savouring 'today' needs to be more important than preparing for 'tomorrow'. It's a bit like switching channels to watch Wimbledon and the Bill—you tend to miss the best bits of both!

Using Photos to Make a Real Small World

(2¹/₂–4 years)

Why we like it

This is an activity that evolved by accident. Some 2 and 3 year olds were getting frustrated because their wooden houses and figures kept falling over on the carpet. This activity presented a solution, which I've tried several times since and it is always very popular.

What you might need

Masking tape or parcel tape

Table mats of all sizes and coasters

Wooden blocks and small sturdy cardboard boxes

Velcro squares

Plasticene

Photos of local shops and buildings or pictures cut from catalogues

Small world people, cars animals, etc.

Useful Tips

Put a knob of Plasticine in the cardboard boxes if they wobble.

Put a small square of peel and stick velcro, felt or blu tac on the back of the photographs so that they can easily be fastened to blocks or boxes that have also had this treatment.

Store all the pictures in a drawer and let the children choose the ones they need as they develop their play.

How you can do it

Use wide masking tape (parcel tape would do just as well unless the children are playing on a priceless rug), and stick down lengths of it at different angles across a carpeted floor. Put table mats at the ends of these 'roads'. The children can choose which photos they want to use to make their town. You may need to help the children fasten the photos to the wood blocks and to lay out their parcel tape roadway, but then sit back and enjoy observing the variety of play you see.

Some children go for careful accuracy, some design an imaginary town, some are only interested in their own home and some are more involved in designing a car park.

What next?

If you work with children who come from far away by car you could try relating this activity to landmarks near your setting.

Create your environment with photographs of local landmarks

Snapshot

Two 3 year olds are playing on a 'tape roadway':
'This is my road. I live here (moving the mat)... And you live round that corner.'
'And here's where the shops are.'
'And the bus goes down there.'
What was impressive was that these two children showed clearly that they were reproducing their own home area with great accuracy, and they started to comment on the lack of props for this:
'We haven't got a Post Office.'
'Or even a Londis.' (said gloomily).
'So, NO SWEETS.' (said in a raised voice intimidating an adult).
I set about thumbing through a local colour supplement for possible pictures, but realised I would only get *their* Londis, park, pillar box, library, etc., if we went out and photographed them.

Making Boats, Cars and Trains

(1–3 years)

Why we like it

Cardboard boxes of all shapes and sizes make wonderful playthings. Besides being free, and easily replaced when they begin to break, you can provide any number, so that very young children who do not yet understand sharing (or even much about taking turns until they are around 4) can play contentedly alongside one another, and will 'notch' this up as something they enjoy doing and want to do again.

What you might need

Shallow strong tomato boxes from the local supermarket make a good starting point, and they can be stacked up in very little space at the end of the day.

50 cm of soft sash cord from a DIY store.

Useful Tips

Supermarket grapefruit boxes are also very strong and have useful holes ready made.

Using a Stanley knife, you can easily give the boxes sloping or curved sides, or an opening door.

How you can do it

1. Thread the cord through the existing hole at the end of the box and knot the ends. This will allow the box to be pulled along easily indoors or out, when full of blocks or toys. This type of box is big enough for a 2 or 3 year old to sit in, and shallow enough for a 1 year old to scramble into.

2. More pieces of sash cord can be used to link several boxes together to form a train; 2 year olds often prefer it not to move—that way they know where they are in relation to you.

Snapshot

Alina (2 years 5 months) approached the line of 7 tomato boxes strung together to form a train. She watched attentively as several confident 3 year olds filled the boxes with purses, plastic food and 'blankets' to go on holiday. She approached the last box, carefully removed the plastic pear and turned the box over before sitting astride it facing the opposite way. There was a slight pause when this was noticed by the other children before Thomas said, 'This is a riding horses holiday' and promptly reversed the first box at the other end and bounced up and down making clip-clopping noises. 3 others followed suit and Alina rode backwards all the way!

Spotlight

Under threes love using these boxes as cars or boats, with cardboard plates and a few cushions or wooden blocks left nearby for them to improvise seats or steering wheels—although often the most successful play is the simplest, with just 'brrrming' noises and hand actions providing the realism.

Letting one thing stand for something else is a part of play that gets easily lost in our world of plastic replicas, so it is often best not to provide too much detail but to take the children's lead and enthusiastically pretend along with them.

What next?

Children begin to discuss ideas, and develop these in their play, usually by 4 years old, and carers can greatly help this process by making sure that the children can use odd bits of equipment for ramps, islands and bridges as the train is transformed into a submarine and the car into a fire engine. Car tyres, milk crates, splinter-free planks of wood, and old bed covers can all be managed by the children themselves as long as they have easy access to them.

Baby-friendly Storage for Books

(9 months–3 years)

Why we like it

When babies have recently begun to walk they enjoy any activity that involves taking things from one place or person to another. Holding the goods tightly, or pushing them in a cart gives them a reason for toddling to and fro on their own 2 feet, gaining admiration from their carers and practising their new skill at the same time.

Combine this urge on the baby's part, with your wish to keep the floor reasonably clear of fallen objects, and you have 2 good reasons for making a book box. This one is the right height for toddlers, will not tip up, and can be personalised.

What you might need

A cardboard wine or grapefruit box, or a box of similar strength and size, is just right for this purpose

Stanley knife

A collection of old photographs, postcards or pictures cut from magazines.

How you can do it

1. Use the Stanley Knife to make the 2 long sides slope down towards the front from approximately quarter of the way along the box.

2. Let the baby rummage through the picture collection to choose some favourites for you to stick on the box. (This may take some time as many babies choose, then chew, then carry their picture around scrunched up in a little hot hand, and so that opportunity passes!)

3. Glue the pictures that you are finally given to the outside of the box, and then place in the books facing the lowest end, so that the fronts can be seen as they are flicked forward.

4. This box is stable on the floor and standing babies as young as 8 or 9 months can hold on to it to retrieve a favourite book to explore.

Snapshot

Evie (14 months) looks towards her book box: 'Book, book! Ace? Ace?'
Childminder: 'Are you going to find a book Evie?'
Evie tugs at several books and pulls 3 onto the floor. She turns them over and picks up one in each hand, but holds out one as she approaches her childminder: 'Acey, Acey'.
Childminder: 'Oh Maisy........'Happy Birthday Maisy'—that's the one you want!'
Evie: 'Cuppa!'
Once on the childminder's lap, Evie turns the pages to find the picture of Maisy having her birthday drink.

What next?

There are dozens of attractive books for babies and toddlers on the market now. Made of card or plastic coated paper, they have high quality illustrations using photographs or realistic drawings. Look for ones that the baby can handle alone, as well as with your help—that is not too big or too heavy—and with just one story in each book. Add home-made books to the collection too, and don't be in too much of a hurry to permanently get rid of books that you think perhaps are outgrown. This is always a temptation as the number of books continues to increase, but babies and toddlers enjoy going back to old favourites from time to time... don't we all?

Making a Dolls House to Take Travelling

(2–4 years)

Why we like it

When 2 and 3 year olds go somewhere new they like to take some familiar things with them.

This dolls house folds easily into a small carrier bag or into the top of a suitcase for travelling. You could 'velcro' the base on to a beanbag lap tray for a child confined to a bed or a wheelchair or even to play with on a long car journey.

What you might need

A box, preferably rectangular with sides that will fit into the base area when folded down. A packing box for a radio, or a large shoebox would be about right

Stanley knife

Tool for punching holes

Ribbon or string

Brown parcel paper

Glue

Scraps of fabric

Pictures

Crayons or felt pens.

Snapshot

Sophie (22 months) had a family of wooden elephant ornaments living in her doll's house, and they went to sleep in a line under a flannel. She found a fish paste jar for their drinks and then filled it with twigs for flowers.

How you can do it

1. With a Stanley knife slit all four corners down to the base. Turn the flattened box over and punch small holes in three of the walls as shown below. Paste brown parcel paper on the outside surfaces to provide added strength. Thread ribbon or string through each hole so that the three walls can be tied together in an upright position (the fourth side can stay down flat as the garden).

2. Turn the box over and glue scraps of wallpaper or gift wrapping paper to the walls. Glue a piece of winter skirt material or an upholstery sample to the floor, and some green felt or a scrap of tweed material on the garden section.

That completes the basics.

Older siblings or visiting children enjoy finding and cutting out photos of windows, pictures, a fireplace, television, clock, mirrors, etc. to stick on to the walls. Flowers, doors and dustbins can be drawn on the outside.

Even very young children will have their own ideas about who lives in the house.

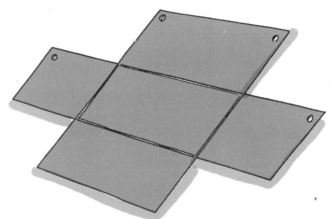

Spotlight

Many 2–3 year olds play imaginatively and contentedly for long periods of time with 'small world' figures and buildings, but there are some points that are worth remembering when providing these for this age.

The first is that it is unrealistic to expect them to share the accommodation, and even those massive dolls houses designed for several children to use in a nursery class often end up as rented rooms! Cars whizzing down a garage ramp, or the joint use of an airport building, can sometimes be co–operatively enjoyed, but not this more personal 'home' play which is essentially a solo play time and very valuable as that. The child needs to be in control of all the roles, and in charge of the action, as well as the manager of the set, and there is rarely room for another adult or child in the play.

The other observation is that a surprising amount of the action seems to take place in the area outside the house or castle—on the balcony, in the garden, down the road—or in just one general room, so this travelling dolls house often meets the child's needs perfectly.

Useful Tips

I've found that improvised furniture is less likely to topple over and frustrate very small children. A coaster or stock cube box makes a good bed with a cotton wool square as the cover, a screw top lid can be a bath and two year olds upwards enjoy picking blades of grass and petals to put in a seashell for food. Children of this age aren't fussy about items being to scale!

 ## What next?

This simple one room arrangement is enjoyed for several more years for playing schools or hospitals or for creating a miniature used car showroom, cafe, garden shed or a shop. As children get older it still helps to make a flattened box that ties up as it is much easier to stick small and intricate parts on the walls that way.

Making a 'Small World' Wild Wood

(2¹/₂–4 Years)

Why we like it

A Wild Wood made from a box can appeal equally to boys and girls. It can be a place where secret treasure is hidden, or the bears live, or where the Lego children end up spending the night when they missed the boat home. Caring and sharing dramas for boys to act out in their own way can be few and far between, but a Wild Wood can provide some—mixed with a bit of testosterone excitement!

Spotlight

From a very early age boys and girls like playing with cars, wooden railways, fire engines, garages, airports, farms and boats, but in my experience boys play less with a dolls house, where all that 'small world' interacting, eating, sleeping and caring happens. You do not often see those sides of life emerge from the 'nee–naw–gallopy–gallopy–whee–brrm–crash!' scenarios of other 'small world' play!

What you might need

A strong cardboard box (surprise, surprise!). I used a box that had held a microwave oven to make one and a 'book box' from a removal firm for another

Stanley knife

Scissors

PVA Glue

Samples of curtain material printed with leaves, flowers, bamboo, etc.

Cardboard tubes (from paper towels, or the ones that hold a stack of crisps)

Plasticine or similar material

Pipe cleaners for twigs—or use real ones from outside

A torch or bike lamp

How you can do it

1. Cut off most of 1 end of the box and cut another archway in the side or the back to allow the child easy access to the inside.

2. Don't worry about straight edges—the curvier the better.

3. Cut material scraps roughly to fit and stick them with PVA glue on the inside of the box for the forest floor and woods—bubbling and overhanging parts all add to the realism.

4. Spare lengths of fabric can be stuck round the cardboard tubes for trees, and stuck with real, or pipe cleaner, twigs.

5. Push one end of the tube into a lid filled with plasticine for stability. Alternatively just use a few leafy twigs, bend them round to fit in the box and replace them when they droop.

6. Cut another hole in the box for the torch to shine through.

Other props can be improvised as the play develops and soon the children will be devising their own.

Useful Tips

Long life light bulb holders make realistic caves, and a tent can be made out of small square box cut diagonally across.

Egg cosies make good sleeping bags, or these can be made from a rectangle of fleece material, folded roughly into thirds and stitched along the double sides

Scraps of red tissue paper glued in a Marmite lid with some twigs could be the campfire, and a camping metal mirror or a length of blue ribbon can be a lake or river.

Snapshot

Ben (3 years, 10 months) holding an adult male Lego person at the doorway of a cave in the wild wood, talks to a Lego child inside the cave: 'Now you stay in here. I'm going to get some food and if you see a bear, you hide in the sleeping bag. I'll get some food to cook and find some plates.' He moves the adult male person outside the wood, then turns him round and goes back. 'And watch out for the pirates, in case they come. When I come back it will be daytime.' Ben looks round the playroom, finds a cheese box lid and wooden bowl and picks the miniature red baubles off a toy Christmas tree. He arranges these like a meal on the lid inside the wood, then reaches out for the torch and turns it on: 'Boy! Boy! Wake Up! It's daytime now and I've found breakfast for you and I killed the bear, so you can come out.'

What next?

Older children enjoy making these woods for younger ones, and then often make another version for themselves. 9 year old Jake made one, complete with a shoe box caravan, for his sister's third birthday, and then made a maxi version for himself and his Action Man dolls.

Imitating and Pretending...

...and not a Batman or Turtle insight. Real props for real life. (18 months–4 years)

Why we like it

Babies learn a great deal by imitating adults, and we encourage this by sometimes putting their feelings into words ourselves.

Toddlers quickly become so skilled at imitating that they can often characterise a person or pet with just one action or prop as, for instance, Charlie (2 years, 2 months) who approaches the day nursery carer on all fours and gently headbutts her shin. Stroking Charlie's hair the carer says: 'Oh hello little cat, would you like a saucer of milk?'

What you might need

Real props—special child sized props don't necessarily help this age group to feel like mum or dad or the postman—only to feel dressed up

Collect old wallets, purses, handbags, clocks, watches, hats, gloves, slip-on shoes, old keys and keyrings

Ask friends and neighbours or local firms to see if they have any discarded hats or badges, or perhaps an old keyboard or cardboard photo of last year's model of computer

1 or 2 small publicity cards from local firms often displayed at the exit of DIY stores make good credit cards

Bus, train, air and cinema tickets, and small change left over from a holiday which, with a few 2p pieces, is more realistic than plastic or cardboard money

A wooden spoon, a small metal saucepan and a stainless steel tea or coffee pot that can double as a kettle are more convincing than plastic pots and pans. Plastic replica food is a useful standby but try adding a dish of sultanas and chopped apple or carrot for a bit of realism sometimes

A sheet of airmail stickers or some old Christmas stickers make excellent stamps for letters to post.

How you can do it

What exactly it is in the looks, behaviour or speech of mum or dad, the doctor or the next door neighbour that makes that person different from anybody else, is a very valuable part of learning. How grandad whistles without a tune, or the postman moves the gate with his foot, or what a horse does that distinguishes it from a cow, and vice versa, all get closely observed and then copied.

The real world is exciting enough for under 4s without needing to add any fantasy creatures or figures. Toddlers and young children who imitate the behaviour of actual people and animals in their everyday life will gradually group all this experience together to create pretend situations in their play.

The youngest children will enjoy your company in their play as long as you follow their lead and willingly pretend to go to sleep or drink endless cups of tea.

Follow their lead and pretend to drink endless cups of tea

Snapshot

Jumilla (3 years, 7 months) puts grass and pebbles into a saucepan:
'I'm the mummy and I cook the dinners, so... 'Dinner time!' Go and get washed, and you eat a little bit Baysey.'
Baysey (3 years, 4 months): 'I'm not Baysey. I'm the dad, and I've got to go out with my taxi so give me three Hobnobs and my flask please mummy.'
Jumilla: 'Alright, there you are. I'll lid your dinner for later, bye.'
Baysey: 'Bye,and you can take Baysey to Whizz Kids later, Bye.'

('lidding the dinner' was, from Jumilla's actions, covering it to warm through later.)

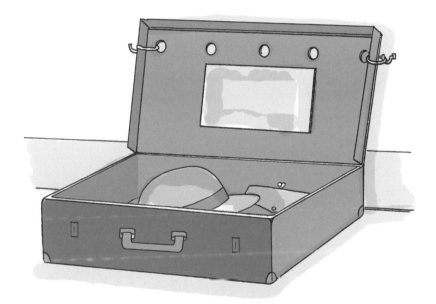

Useful Tips

You could try storing all the props in an old hard-topped suitcase, or shallow trunk with a few holes drilled in the lid. Tie a loop of strong string, or a short length of basin chain with a plug on one end, through the holes at each end of the lid to fasten to cup hooks on the wall behind. This will hold the lid securely open. You could glue an unbreakable mirror to the inside of the lid. When not in use the case makes an extra seat or a kneeling height play top.

Spotlight

As the children reach 3 years or so they get ideas for developing their own pretend play by rummaging through the props and so need to access to a range of them.

Sometimes you might show them new possibilities, for example, making a card shop in the New Year, or a theatre after a trip to the pantomime, but most of all they enjoy putting their own interpretations on everyday events that happen in their familiar world. This is invaluable for helping them to understand that different people see the same thing differently!

What next?

Pretending can be enjoyed by a wide age range of children and a collection of props is a wonderful resource in a family centre or a setting that welcomes children of different ages. If you are catering for older ones they will enjoy dressing in particular outfits from all cultures, but under 4s are often happiest with a collection of hats and shoes plus 1 or 2 metre lengths of material that they can wrap around and fasten with a velcro strip. These can be used as cloaks, skirts or bedcovers as they like.

Doll Play Matters... for Babies, Girls, and Boys

(1–4 years)

Why we like it

A sitting baby will stare and poke at facial features of a doll, smiling, patting and vocalising at it in recognition. A small soft doll is often the first toy to be hugged and carried round, and later covered up or wrapped in a cloth.

It is from about 16–18 months old that doll play really begins to develop and it provides children, up to about 4 years old, with an opportunity to be 'big' and 'in charge' just at a time when they may feel they don't have as much power as they would like. However in order to enjoy these powerful feelings the child needs to feel older than the doll, so the doll's shape and features need to be those of a younger child or a baby. The child also needs to be able to handle the doll easily—it is hard to enjoy being the grown-up if you can hardly pick up the 'baby'.

These dolls are all less than a foot high

What you might need

A number of dolls of suitable size (a good rule of thumb for the doll's height is for it to match floor to knee of the child) and lightweight with suitably 'baby' or small child features

Some male and some female dolls

Dolls with different eye, skin, hair colour and facial features so that all children can identify with them

Some teddies, Teletubbies and soft animals for children who relate more easily to these

Some dolls that can be bathed without taking forever to stop leaking

Clothes with simple Velcro fastenings (very fiddly clothes are enjoyed by some 5–9 year olds but they just frustrate younger children)

Floor to knee of the child's height

How you can do it

Provide choice and a range of props that the child might use with the doll. It is worth remembering that children of this age often use the doll to act out their own conflicts with carers, but in this play the child is of course the grown up. Children aged 1 to 4 are at a stage when their choices are somewhat restricted and sometimes hard for them to understand, such as, too big for a bottle or nappy, too small to cross the road or stay up late. Sorting out these conflicts with a doll helps their understanding.

Some children relate more easily to soft animals

Here are a few examples:

About bedtime

You might provide a torch or battery-powered touch lamp, a bed or cot (shoe boxes do well), 2 or 3 small picture books, a dummy, bottle, tiny teddy or other items associated with bedtime.

About mealtimes

You might provide a cup, bowl, spoons, some real food and perhaps a highchair for the doll. A section of a small box fastened to an adult chair makes a very satisfactory highchair.

Too small to cross the road

About potty training, bathtime or jealousy of a new baby

Just improvise whatever is needed, using plastic mugs (for potties), washing up bowls (for baths), or a small woven basket (for a baby's cradle).

Spotlight

Doll play is a form of play that has greatly changed in recent years as toy manufacturers have produced more and more sophisticated replicas of fantasy figures and teenage dolls of impossible proportions with pre-programmed electronic phrases that prevent children from 'owning' the doll and using it in *their* way. But there are still a range of very appropriate dolls for those under four years in good toyshops and by mail order if you search around.

Sometimes, perhaps especially by boys who may not have been given a doll to play with very much, a toy animal or teddy or Teletubby with its baby shape and features, is favoured over a doll and becomes an essential companion at bedtime.

Snapshot

Dina (2 years and 8 months old) has a 6-week old baby brother at home. She was encouraged by the day nursery staff to take some baby doll play items into the willow house in the garden. A member of staff, sitting with her back to the house recorded the following conversation.

'Oh, you baby, baby, just crying and crying. You're a bad baby eating mummy's boobies. You hurting mummy and waking up Dini and daddy. You go way and be Dini's baby now in the woods. And you have Dini's dum-dum. Dini's a big girl now and Dini sing you' She sings "We will rock you, rock you, rock you". Now you good baby and sleeps.'

The staff were sensitive in keeping back and observing unobtrusively, and were able to pass on this observation to Dina's mum who could reassure her daughter that she wasn't being eaten!

What next?

If the child seems unnecessarily aggressive with a doll don't worry and, still less, interfere!

The enjoyment of being the 'big person' begins with realising what you are able to do if you want to. This is an important element of play and 'Oh poor, poor dolly' from an adult doesn't help the process.

Finding out that when you are big you can stamp on an ant, and probably do on a few, is followed by understanding that you could, but you don't have to. Later still comes the understanding that power means you can protect something vulnerable. This whole process will be worked through over varying lengths of time as children watch carefully how the adults around them use *their* powers.

'Allo 'Allo

Talking and listening on a home-made telephone (2–4 years)

Why we like it

The give and take of conversation takes a lot of practice, and we often find ourselves worrying about a young child that isn't speaking enough or another that never stops talking! Saying something, then pausing to listen to someone else before saying some more is, like all turn-taking a very difficult skill for small children.

This home-made phone is cheap to make and can be used to connect children with their carers or friends over short or longer distances, indoors or out.

What you might need

2 plastic funnels from a DIY store

A length of hose pipe (an old one that you are replacing will do and any length can be used up to about 4 m)

A reel of elastoplast or electrician's tape

A Stanley knife.

How you can do it

Cut the required length of hose pipe and insert a funnel into each end. If the hose is too narrow to do this easily, make 1 or 2 short slits lengthways at each end until you can get the funnels in. Secure them by binding the elastoplast tightly round the join.

2 year olds playing with the telephone find it hard to move from listening to speaking, so they enjoy this game best if they can see you and can nod or shake their heads in reply to what they hear. Then show them how to speak and you respond in the same way.

They enjoy this game best if they can nod or shake their head in reply

Later on they will get the idea of moving the funnel from ear to mouth and back again, and will enjoy communicating with friends between two rooms, over a ground floor window sill, under a blanket, over a sofa or between two tents or dens such as cardboard boxes.

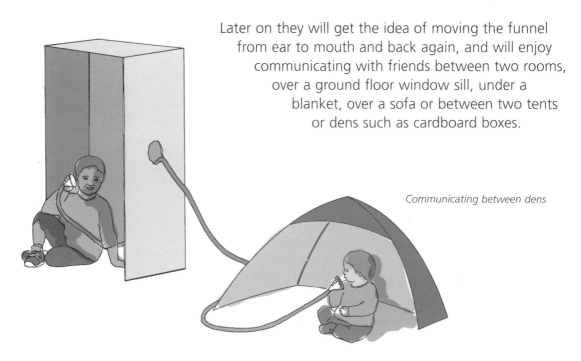

Communicating between dens

What next?

The home-made phone can be used for a listening game. Place the hose pipe over a ground floor window sill or run it through a doorway to the next room, and put one end on the floor or a low table. The child at this end chooses some different sounds to make, for example:

Banging 2 teaspoons together

Swishing some water

Singing a nursery rhyme

Jingling some keys

Winding up a toy

The child at the other end listens carefully and tells you what they can hear. If the child has had a bad cold and you suspect that there may be deafness in one ear, you can test this further by encouraging listening with the left and then to the right ear.

Snapshot

During the summer some toddlers with a local childminder had a wonderful time in the garden with home-made phones draped around the bushes. They then filled a jug and small watering can with water from the outside tap, poured it carefully into one funnel and squealed with delight as the water came out of the other end. With a bit of judicious moving of the hose, several plants got watered at the same time.

Dens, the Play We All Remember

(1 year onwards)

Why we like it

Finding or making a den and then playing in it seems to be an instinctive activity for children anywhere in the world... and for parents too, when you watch them 'bag' a bit of beach, put a windbreak round and the towels down! It is possible to provide all sorts of dens that give enormous enjoyment, and opportunities to watch the world go by, without spending much money at all. This activity suggests some of the possibilities for dens indoors.

What you might need

Depending on the space and number of dens, a selection of the following:

Old sheets or bedspreads

Strong scissors

A hole punch (an eyelet punch kit is the best as each hole has a rivet and re-enforcers and will last much longer)

Packet of large plastic covered cup hooks

A camping washing line, sash cord or strong string

Double sided tape and roll of wallpaper border

Large cardboard boxes and a Stanley knife

Cushions, blankets or rugs, fleeces, etc.

Wooden blocks (especially long ones).

How you can do it

Provide several types of dens if you have a number of children of different ages. Some 3 year olds may use the den as a camp for several friends but others, and certainly the younger ones, will enjoy having their own space without any pressure to share it. They also need the opportunity to 'own' their den long enough for some really satisfying play... this isn't a 'five minutes each' situation like a turn on a wagon or trike!

Put an old double sheet over a full size table so that the edges touch the floor on 3 sides. If the sheet is really old you could cut 1 or 2 portholes in it. Secure it to the table with a giant bulldog clip or place a car rug over the table top to make it less inclined to slip.

Upturn a low table or coffee table for use as a boat. Lash soft toys to the top of each leg for safety, and keep watch of course!

Pull out the sofa at an angle to the wall, and make a third wall with a pile of cushions.

Sweet-talk an electrical retailer for a 'fridge container', or a removal firm for some big boxes they are about to discard. Cut off one of the short sides, and make some peep holes with a Stanley knife.

Fasten a batten with several cup hooks screwed to it along one wall of your playroom about 1 m 50 cm off the ground. Make eyelets along the length of an old sheet and hook these on to the cuphooks. Create a space between the wall and sheet with pillows or cushions on the inside and wooden blocks on the outside edge of the sheet. Of course you can create 2 or 3 little tents this way.

If you screw a similar batten on the opposite wall and thread a washing line between them, you can create a series of tunnels and gaps across the room which cause great giggling and scurrying at almost any age.

Mark out some individual spaces on the floor using a roll of wallpaper border, leaving gaps for doorways. Toddlers find this space, with perhaps a doll, a cover and a cushion, a very satisfying way of playing alongside other toddlers with identical provision in their 'houses' (you could also make the houses with circles of wooden blocks). Young children enjoy having a snack in any of these dens, and playing 'bedtime' with a torch and a cover.

Snapshot

A grandma recently moved to a semi-furnished flat complete with a round ceiling canopy and full-length curtains over a massive double bed. The double bed went to a good home but the canopy wasn't wanted, and was still in place when the grandchildren made their first visit. The new layout, interesting balcony, familiar and unfamiliar items only got a cursory glance. Round eyed and excited they appeared from that bedroom: 'Mum, mum—gran's got an indoor tent to play in!'

A secret place away from eveyone else

Spotlight

A den is your own little shelter away from everyone else, a 'secret' place to be on your own and play in your own way.

But it is also a place where you can watch what is happening outside without getting involved. Children of all ages enjoy this 'onlooker' play very much and learn a lot from it.

It is sometimes hard to provide onlooker play in a busy care setting or centre for families. For babies these safe, watching times happen from their carer's lap or hip, or in a highchair or in those big old-style prams in the garden or when out for a walk. As the baby becomes a toddler, the highchair is often replaced by a low group table, and the big pram by a buggy with its dismal views of the bottom of walls, legs and car exhausts. Suddenly onlooker play opportunities are in rather short supply, and many day care practitioners are concerned about this.

What next?

Here are some examples of how daycare settings have developed this activity.

A family centre has very successfully provided a sloping pathway along the playroom wall with a platform at the end and wooden banisters all along. Toddling babies clamber up and contentedly peer at their peers, as well as being able to see out of the windows.

This could be equally workable in a childminder's house or any setting where the windows are not at a toddler friendly height.

A work place nursery centre has gone even further by creating a similar walkway with several small shelters at intervals round two walls of their very small outdoor area. Accessible and safe, it provides solo and group den play for 2–5 year olds.

A day nursery which has a large expanse of grass has used the services of a local willow weaver to plant a coiling willow maze with several exits and entrances, and a magical leafy 'room' in the middle.

Safety Check

Check window catches are child safe.

Familiar Things in Suprising Places

(18 months–4 years)

Why we like it

This chapter is all about being unconventional and showing children that it is fine to be so. Toddlers settle to play best when they recognise most of their playthings, so for these youngest children encouraging a fresh approach might involve putting favourite things in a different place.

What you might need

Consider almost anything that you have in your setting, or that you are thinking of discarding. Does it have potential for use in another way?

Safety Check

When adapting anything old, or that hasn't been made for that specific purpose, be especially careful to check for safety hazards such as sharp edges, loose small parts, splinters, etc. Plastic bags of any type are never playthings.

How you can do it

Here are just a few improvisations that have been enjoyed by under fours.

Guttering on the stairs makes a great slide for dolls and teddies. Several lengths of it can be used to set up a bouncy ball run, or outside as a waterfall down into a baking tin.

A plastic cat litter tray or dog bed, well disinfected, or an outgrown baby bath, makes an excellent sand or water tray for a 1 or 2 year old. If placed directly on the ground so that the toddler can squat next to it, surprisingly little sand or water gets split.

Filling and pouring water with small metal jugs or teapots, or adding water to sand or earth to make a muddy mix are two popular activities.

An old spoon or dinner fork can be used with soft earth to make holes for small plants, which can then be watered. This is enjoyed by 2, 3 and 4 year olds.

An old lorry tyre, hosed down, and painted if you like, makes a strong wall for a sandpit that is comfortable to sit on too. A friendly tyre centre will usually cut a worn car tyre in half around the perimeter to make two circular canals for floating leaves or small boats.

Going tottin' ('rag and boning' or playing 'Yipyan`, depending on where you live) is one of my favourite activities for 1–4 year olds. Just make a heap of scarves, hats, cushions, baskets, small world people and animals, shoes and dolls—or something from every activity in this book if you like. Then invite the children to go and rummage. It's fascinating to see the combination of items that they choose, and the way they play with them.

Spotlight

A worker in a day nursery wanted to encourage hunting and gathering skills for a toddler in her care whose favourite toy was a box of farm animals.

She brought in a multi-coloured patchwork jacket and laid it out on the floor with the arms outstretched and the buttons done up. She then placed the farm animals in the sleeves, pockets, under the collar and between the buttons leaving one cow's head showing. Winston (17 months old) found, replaced and lined up the animals with great concentration for almost half an hour. He then scrambled into the jacket himself, flapping the arms with delight. This activity's success was the result of the nursery worker recognising Winston's preference for particular playthings, as well as his need for a greater challenge. Sometimes putting a new item, such as an improvised bridge with the road layout, will cause a swift development of the play.

From about 2 years old children benefit from being with adults who show them new ways to use familiar things. They learn to improvise by seeing their carers do this, and they get great satisfaction from taking something, perhaps that is no longer needed, and using it in a different way. If 2–3 year olds are praised for their good ideas they will gain self-confidence and rarely be bored as these incidental discoveries made by the child often lead to long and satisfying play times.

Snapshot

A row of old hats kept 2 and 3 year olds with their childminder happily engaged as they threw screwed-up paper balls into them. The hats got used again after tea, but turned the other way up, to guess where the toy rabbit was hiding.

The childminder recorded the children's ability to give verbal clues, from the oldest (3 years and 10 months): 'The rabbit likes furry hats', others in the group commented 'He likes racing caps' and 'His bestest hat is the blue one', and Eddie the youngest (2 years and 5 months) pointed and said 'He's in there!'

What next?

Some of the best inventions have been made by people who were surprised by what they saw and applied it to something else. If we encourage children to be inventive by wondering out loud 'I wonder what would happen if...?' they will see that it is alright not to know the answer, and will be more likely to 'have a go'. It might not always result in Stephenson's Rocket or the discovery of penicillin, but who knows where that enquiry will lead them!

Keeping it All together When Out and About

tabards for babies and toddlers (6 months–2 years)

Why we like it

When travelling with children their safety is paramount and their contentment is closely linked with your ability to concentrate on driving, or on crossing the road with the buggy and shopping. This tabard is very quick to make and ensures that all comfort objects stay safely within grasp.

What you might need

An oblong of non-fraying fleece or similar material

If you buy 90 cm wide you'll only need about 30 cm for each tabard if the design on the material will go sideways

2 brass 2 cm curtain rings

90 cm of satin ribbon cut in half

2–3 good quality key rings, also about 2 cm diameter

Strong thread

For the two part version, you will also need 2 x 10 cm lengths of hook and loop sew-on velcro to join the two halves at the shoulders.

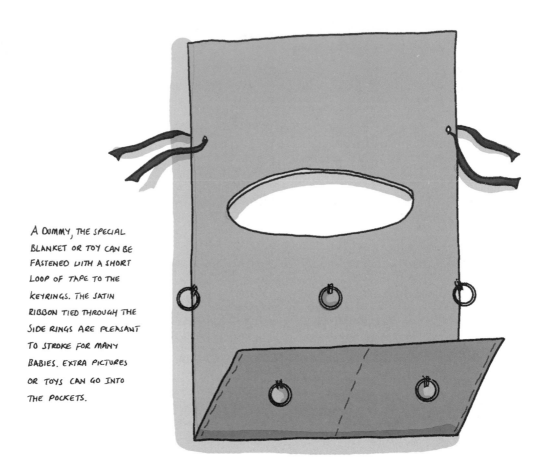

A DUMMY, THE SPECIAL BLANKET OR TOY CAN BE FASTENED WITH A SHORT LOOP OF TAPE TO THE KEYRINGS. THE SATIN RIBBON TIED THROUGH THE SIDE RINGS ARE PLEASANT TO STROKE FOR MANY BABIES. EXTRA PICTURES OR TOYS CAN GO INTO THE POCKETS.

How you can do it

You can make this tabard with just one oblong of material the width of the child's shoulders, longer in the front to allow you to turn up a pocket, and with a hole cut to fit over the child's head.

If the tabard is in two halves, illustrated below, it doesn't need to be pulled over the child's head. It can be adjusted to fit as the child gets bigger by using the full length of the velcro strips.

Sew a brass curtain ring on either side of the front section to come below the child's arms.

Sew, or make a hole and tie, a length of satin ribbon on the back section opposite the rings, to tie the tabard together.

Sew up the sides of the front pocket.

Sew 2 or 3 keyrings anywhere on the front of the tabard, on which to tie the child's 'must haves'

Spotlight

Cars, like all road safety issues, need all child carers to apply consistent ground rules, and parents may be grateful for the support of childcare workers in helping to establish these. Parents fetching their child at the end of the day feel fraught and guilty if getting into the car causes an upset child. Sitting on the adult's lap or in the front seat 'just down the road' is plain dangerous and can set up months, if not years, of arguments of the 'you-let-me-last-time' or 'this-is-a-quiet-road' type when setting out on every journey. It is worth establishing that these rules don't budge even if it means going back indoors sometimes to make the point.

Some toddlers get quite adept at wriggling out of the car seat harness and again it is worth stopping the car every time. If you make the two-part tabard it is possible to fasten the front over the car seat harness which might help. It may help in the same way when using a buggy or a supermarket trolley.

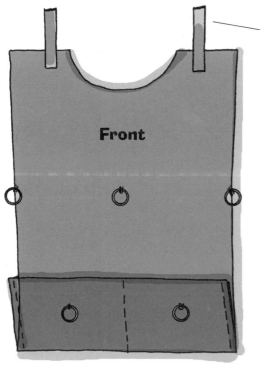

LOOPSIDE OF VELCRO FACING DOWNWARDS, AND ONLY 2 CM SEWN ON TO THE FRONT TO ALLOW FOR ADJUSTMENT

HOOKSIDE OF VELCRO UPPERMOST, SEWN FULLY ON TO THE BACK

Front

Back

What next?

Song and story tapes that are not too jangling are invaluable for most car journeys with small children. You can join in without turning round—showing an interest without having to make eye contact!

Fastening the middle seat belt through slits at one end of a cardboard box can be invaluable for keeping a selection of things within reach of two children in the back of a vehicle.

As children get older, bean bag lap trays can be useful for supporting drawings and books.

Party Fun

(For 1, 2 and 3 year olds)

Why we like it

Parties for children who have just turned 3 and those who are younger, can be great fun for them and their carers, if you are able to keep things simple, small and familiar. 'The same number of children as the child is years old' is a good rule of thumb for a manageable size from the child's point of view, but often this turns out to be impossible and before you know it, the local hall and the bouncy castle is booked, and everyone feels tearful! Here are some pick and mix ideas that may help about games, timing and food.

What you might need

1, 2 and just 3 year olds enjoy games which are non-competitive with everyone a winner every time! Apart from Pass the Parcel, stick to clapping for winning

For a selection of games you'll need:

Hats (2 more than the number of children)

Cushions or a book of carpet samples from a local shop (2 more than the number of children)

Some cut out old birthday cards or sheets of coloured or origami paper

A simple tape player, or a confident pianist and piano

A colour dice (either home-made using a square wooden brick, or one from a board game).

How you can do it

Musical Mats or Cushions can be played by all children once they can toddle about. Dance round until the music stops then find a cushion or a mat. Everyone claps for the one who is on the mat nearest to the door, or with the red pattern, etc. Continue until everyone has had a clap, without removing any cushions so that everyone can play right through.

A Hunting Game can be played by 1 and 2 year olds. The children search the room or garden for the cut–out birthday card pictures. Most will need adult support and will want to keep their cards. For 3 year olds, use several sheets of coloured or origami paper at once to cut out lots of copies of 2 objects with a simple outline (for example, a car and a ball) and hide these fairly obviously round the room or garden. Toss the dice and all look for a red ball or a green car, etc. Lots of claps and help for everyone to find objects—make sure you have cut out loads to start off with!

Pass the Hat can be played by 1 and 2 year olds. Dance and when the music stops find/ choose a hat from the ones spread round the room. Clap for the two children wearing policemen's hats, etc.

For 3 year olds, have enough hats for everyone to have one. Pass them round as the music plays, and when it stops, put on the one you are holding. (This always causes lots of laughter, so you maybe be able to take a rest from the clapping!)

Pass the Parcel works well for a 3 year old's birthday party. You'll need as many parcels as there are children with an identical toy in the middle of each. When the music stops everyone takes a layer off the parcel they are holding until finally the music stops, the prizes are revealed, and everyone is a winner.

Spotlight

Just Threes and children who are younger do not yet understand about sharing and this is not bad manners but an ancient instinct that helped young humans to survive in more desperate times in our earliest history. Today, with luck, they will sing 'Happy Birthday to You' and with support they'll let the birthday child blow out the candles, but that is quite enough generosity for one party!

Safety Check

Bits of balloon have a nasty habit of sticking over windpipes, so blow bubbles are best for parties with this age group.

Timing and Food

Many 1–3 year olds are shy of taking food that is passed to them, so for a birthday tea it can work better to put a selection of things (for example, some cubes of cheese and apple, raisins, slices of banana, crisps and a cup cake with a toy standing on the icing) in a party cardboard dish or a decorated cake box for each child. This also means you can adjust the contents for a particular child who has an allergy to certain foods, for instance.

It doesn't have to be an afternoon party—candles and cake can be served at any time so, would a lunch time party be better, with games in the garden, and beans and mash to eat?

Toddlers who are dropping asleep by midday might enjoy a 10–11.30am party with croissants and sliced bananas mid-morning and then some birthday fun before everyone needs a nap.

If many guests need to be invited, several small gatherings over a few days, or even over the course of one day, might be easier with quieter and more energetic sessions to suit the different children invited at different times.

Many 1–3 year olds are shy of taking food that is passed to them by unfamiliar adults

Spotlight

Try to have as many adults as children for this age group, to care for children needing help, cuddles or the loo, as well as helping with food and supporting games.

A brightly coloured sticker or toy to take home at the end will be very popular but go easy on artificially brightly coloured food. It doesn't make sense to serve food on a happy occasion that is going to mean that some children won't be able to cope or enjoy the party.

What next?

Older children, for instance with a childminder, in a family centre or on a playscheme, like to be consulted and often to be involved in planning a party for younger ones. Would they enjoy decorating the table, helping with games, reading a story or being the photographer?

And have a great time!